a SHRIMP, COLLARDS & GRITS *cookbook*

# PULLIN' POTS
*Southern Blue Crab, Recipes & Lowcountry Lore*

**PAT BRANNING**

*Southern Lifestyle Series*

# SHRIMP, COLLARDS & GRITS

**PULLIN'POTS** - Southern Blue Crab, Recipes & Lowcountry Lore

**Shrimp, Collards & Grits Southern Lifestyle Series**
*Copyright © 2016 by Branning Publishing, Inc; original written content & photographs only.*

www.shrimpcollardsgrits.com

Copyright © 2016 artists as identified
All original artwork reproduced in this publication.

Copyright © 2016 Andrew Branning
All original photos reproduced in this publication except Adobe stock images.

**International Standard Book Number: 978-0-9896340-6-9**

All rights reserved. No portion of this book may be reproduced, stored in a retrieval system, or transmitted in any form or by any means mechanical, electronic, photocopying, recording, or otherwise-without prior written permission from the publisher, except as provided by United States of America copyright law.

Published by Branning Publishing, Inc.
www.branningpublishing.com

Printed in China.

# CONTENTS

**SOUTHERN BLUE CRAB &**
**LOWCOUNTRY LORE  10**

**Gullah Fixin's  18**
Shout Hallelujah Crab Fried Rice  20
Crab, Shrimp and Okra Gumbo  23

**Appetizers for Autumn Gatherings  24**
Isle of Palms Crab Dip  25
Savannah Crab Mornay Dip  30
Colleton Crab Melts  34
Crab and Corn Fritters  36
Sea Island Crab Au Gratin  38
Charlie's Crab Stuffed Shrimp  41
Charleston's Meeting Street Crab  42
Tybee Crab and Artichoke Dip  45
Savory Crabmeat Cheesecake  46
Sandlapper Crabmeat Hush Puppies  48

**Crab Cakes and the Prince of Tides  50**
Pat Conroy's Crab Cakes with Caper Sauce  52
Jumbo Lump Crab Cakes  55
Crisfield Crab Burgers  56

**Here Come the Succulent Soft Shells  58**
Deep-Fried Soft-Shell Crabs  64
Tideland Sautéed Soft- Shell Crabs  67

**Crabtastic Suppers!  70**
Baked Grouper with Lump Crab and Creamy Lemon Grits  71
Rolled Flounder Stuffed with Crab  74
Deep South Crab Pie  76
Seafood Mac and Cheese  78
Crustless Sandlapper Crab Quiche  79
Confederate Crab Imperial  80
Grilled Crab and Cheese Sandwiches  82
Deviled Crab  84
Sullivan's Island Omelet with Crabmeat and Gruyère  85
Spaghetti with Crab and Tomatoes  86

**Thanksgiving by the Sea  90**
Crab Norfolk  92
Butternut Squash Soup with Blue Crab  95
Dora's Rustic Okra Soup with Blue Crab  96
Mrs. Rhett's She-Crab Soup  99

**Special Thanks  102**

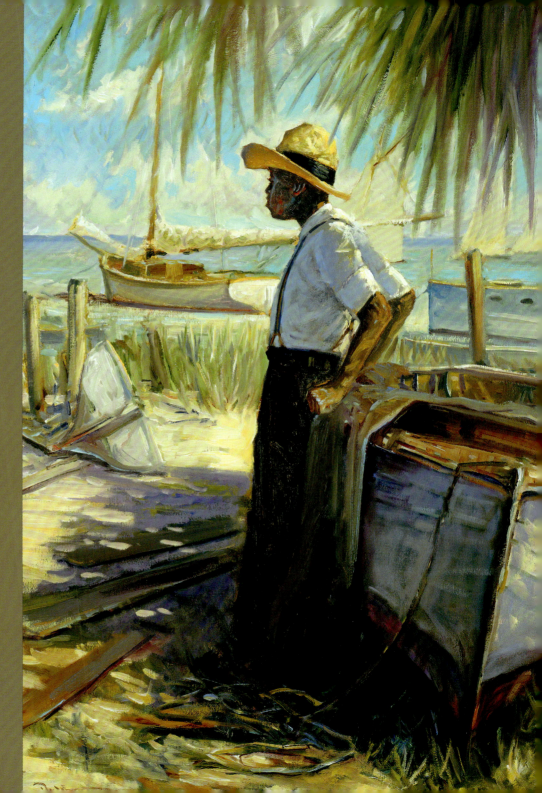

*Call of the Sea*, oil on canvas by John Carroll Doyle.

*We celebrate our* **White Boot Heroes** *who work tirelessly to bring us the bounty of the sea, our rivers and streams. May they continue to serve up the best of our region.*

# Salt Air, Distant Islands & Marshlands

## St. Helena Island, South Carolina

# SOUTHERN BLUE CRAB & LOWCOUNTRY LORE

Neither high winds nor cold drizzle falling at 5 a.m. could stop Craig Reaves as he fires up the diesel engine on his battered 21-foot aluminum boat. He and his brother, Cameron, are already a couple hours into their workday, both seasoned watermen, when they board their craft. Craig bustles about the open vessel, checking the engines and the gear. At last, he pulls in the lines that secure the craft to the weather-worn pier on St. Helena Island, and eases out of the slip.

His routine on this spring morning is one Craig has performed countless times to go crabbing. . "You pretty much need to have it in your blood – grow up around it to really understand it," he says of the waterman's life in his soft-spoken accent. "It's what I always wanted to do, - follow in my father's footsteps."

Today, demand for crabmeat has never been stronger. But the industry is being pinched on a number of fronts, including from a younger generation reluctant to take up the call, an industry reeling from a flood of foreign crabmeat and from conservationists who warn that the crab population is threatened by over-harvesting.

*Culinary guru, John Martin Taylor says in Hoppin' John's Lowcountry Cooking that the crabs of Beaufort County are the finest of the fine. "As much as I love Charleston and Edisto," he writes, "something dramatic happens when you cross Port Royal Sound, a culinary boundary as real as the geographic Fall Line."*

But on this day, Craig is not concerned about such matters. It's the tide, high winds and fouling seas he must think about. Undaunted by the weather, or the tidal pulls, Craig heads out full throttle toward the Broad River. Waves are beginning to break over the bow. Once they arrive at their destination, Craig knows he must climb forward and slip onto the deck of the boat to cast his traps. While the craft bounces and rolls, Craig keeps himself low and eases forward. Once on the bow he grabs one of the wire mesh traps and tosses it into the churning green waters. After a while even the strongest back feels the strain of setting 35- pound crab pots into the water.

The life of a waterman is rugged and often treacherous but there are moments when these waterways, rivers and marshlands rise up and steal your soul. These fishermen take a lot of risk, but theirs is a life of many freedoms. No cubicles to have to work within, no walls around them or rules over their heads. Their livelihood depends only on the strength of their faith, the weather, the crabs and the market.

## Lowcountry Life

Our majestic salt marshes, muddy flats, inviting barrier islands, winding creeks and miles of sandy beaches captivate all who live here and those who simply wish they did. Fresh water meets salt water and creeks, marshes and rivers meld with sunshine, changing tides and warm sea breezes. Many who cruise the Ashepoo, the Combahee and the Colleton rivers for pleasure are unaware that right under their bows is a major fishery quietly going about its business. We tend to ignore the crabbers. Perhaps it is because their early hours are not our hours, or the waters they work are for the most part marshy, full of no-see-ums and far removed from our choice cruising grounds. We tend not to think of them unless by chance we have to steer our boat through a forest of bobbing pot buoys. We cruise slowly, praying we will not hit a trap with our propeller.

Traveling down Hwy. 17 south of Charleston, through vast expanses of marshlands, one enters a world seldom experienced. Here is a place so steeped in history, traditions, soulful colors and magical light that surely it must move historians to weep.

Signs on both sides of the road mark centuries old plantations with names like Twickenham, Cherokee, Clarendon and Bonnie Hall. We turn off onto Rivers Road which runs between Hwy. 17 and the town of Yemassee. To our right was Bonnie Hall, a former rice plantation built along the Combahee River in 1732. it's impossible to overstate the influence rice had on the physical bearing and cultural contours of Charleston. Rice from these plantations is what made Charleston the richest city in Colonial America prior to the Civil War.

## Our Gullah Geechee Heritage

To tell the history of the Lowcountry is to tell the story of the Gullah Geechee people. Geechee is another term for Gullah people, the descendants of slaves. Gullah has come to be the accepted name of the islanders in South Carolina, while Geechee refers to the islanders of Georgia. Some scholars suggest the name comes from the Ogeechee River near Savannah, Georgia.

*Crabbing, oil on canvas by John Carroll Doyle.*

*Low Country, oil on canvas by C Ford Riley.*

"I love the marsh," Pat Conroy says, nodding towards a sweep of Spartina grass. "I don't know of any place that smells like this. It's a magnificent smell. It's the smell of where all life comes from. I love that all shrimp, all crab, all oysters are born in the marsh."

About 250 years ago, West Africans shuffled ashore in Charleston and other port cities, a barefoot legion some 100,000 strong. Known for their ability to grow rice, slave traders sought them out because of their honed farming skills. Plantation owners bought many of them because the subtropical climate of the Atlantic Coast was conducive to successful rice production, similar to that of Sierra Leone in West Africa. They arrived in the Lowcountry, a region which extends roughly from Pawley's Island down to Savannah and about 80 miles inland.

The Lowcountry is an area steeped in tradition with a uniqueness that lies in the fact that our food ways were painstakingly carved out of the land and water by these West African people. Brought here from Sierra Leone as slaves they cultivated rice, cotton and indigo on the plantations. With them came their expertise for growing rice. But there's so much more. Not only did the West Africans bring their farming techniques with them they also brought West African products that have since become staples of the Southern diet: peanuts, okra, sweet potatoes, greens, sorghum, peas, tomatoes, and watermelon. Once here, they plied the local waters for seafood.

From the Santee River in South Carolina to Savannah, Georgia, along two hundred miles of coast, the Gullahs still cling to the edge of America. Theirs is a unique culture in the small, remote communities where they have lived for generations. The marsh-lined shores of St. Helena Island are home to one of the largest Gullah populations. Those who leave often find themselves compelled to return to the land of their origins, the land they love.

Dr. Emory Campbell of Hilton Head Island, born into a family of freed slaves, is one who never left. For over twenty years he served as executive director of Penn Center on St. Helena Island. Tucked in the heart of the South Carolina Sea Islands surrounded by great expanses of marshlands and nestled beneath silvery moss-draped limbs of ancient live oaks, Penn Center is the site of the former Penn School, one of the country's first schools for freed slaves. It stands today as one of the most significant African American historical and cultural institutions in existence.

Through his stories and experiences Emory Campbell teaches thousands of visitors each year the story of his people. He leads

*Midday*, oil on canvas by John Carroll Doyle.

the Gullah Heritage Trail Tours and reflects on his culturally rich past. "Hilton Head was isolated. The heat, the mosquitoes and the inconvenience of getting on an island with no bridge kept the Gullah people in their own separate society." For much of his life he never knew white people even existed.

## THE SECRET INGREDIENT IN GULLAH CUISINE

Gullah cuisine is inextricably tied to the land, the sea, and the seasons. "Soul food" such as collard greens, okra and gumbo originated from African cuisine and forms the basis for many Southern meals. No proper Charleston supper tastes complete without a bowl of fluffy rice, a staple of Gullah tables.

Coming up on spring, ingredients like fresh squash, zucchini, and sweet peas will find their way onto plates. Rice and benne seeds make frequent appearances, and locally available seafood plays a starring role in dishes like crab rice, conch stew, and purloos, a one-pot meal of rice and any variety of add-ins such as okra and shellfish, meat and sausage. The secret to all this deliciousness is "the love." When it's made right, it's made with plenty of love.

However, the origins of these dishes goes way back before the arrival of enslaved people to North America in 1619. These dishes and this culture go back thousands of years into West African history. Take, for example, Chef BJ Dennis, a local chef who stepped out of restaurant kitchens to dedicate himself to educating Charleston and its visitors about Gullah cuisine. He is now considered the cuisine's preeminent ambassador. His efforts are recognized as almost a renaissance; not just with the food, but the culture and saving the land of the Gullah people. He's part of a much larger movement to make sure the Gullah people's vital contribution to Charleston culture is not forgotten.

## CHARLESTON CHEF BJ DENNIS

*"If Mama said, 'Go get lunch,' she meant 'go out on the river.'"*

Chef BJ Dennis, a descendent of slaves, embraces his people's Gullah Geechee past to inspire his future. Dennis grew up eating the food of the Lowcountry without thinking too much about it.

*"Grandma always fried up shark steak because she liked it so much,"* he says. *"It wasn't unusual to find someone just walking around downtown peddling deviled crabs, soft shells or fried shrimp."*

His granddaddy told him stories of how they used to grow rice in the ponds out on Daniel Island, and how there used to be black cowboys minding cattle. His family roots run deep into the Lowcountry. His great grandfather ran a boat that ferried folks on and off Daniel Island long before there were any bridges. As he grew older, BJ says this family history became real to him and he's anxious to learn as much as he can. He encourages his grandfather to tell him all about the coconut trees they grew, the goats they raised in the back yard and what food they ate. BJ wants to introduce people to the food he grew up with, the stuff people are eating at home, catching in nearby waters, and cooking in their kitchens and backyards.

*"Local cuisine is the seafood. Local conch, mullet – it's not trash, it's eatin,"* says BJ. *"Crabs, eels, shark, oysters and shrimp, especially the little creek shrimp you can catch by net up in the creeks are what we ate on a daily basis."*

*"If Mama said go get lunch, she meant get out on the river and cast a net for shrimp, or go catch a fish or some blue crabs."*

*"Charleston is progressing, and I love it, but you can't forget*

*where you come from,"* he says. *"Our culture — new people just don't understand it."*

## Pin Point Heritage Museum

History still lingers at the A.S. Varn and Son Crab Factory at Pin Point on Skidaway Island, Georgia. The A.S. Varn and Son Crab Factory closed in 1985, but every Saturday, visitors can tour the original site tucked away on the road from downtown to the Landings.

There was a time when women picked crab there while rocking their babies to sleep in make-do bassinettes crafted from discarded crab pots. On most winter afternoons, men would return from sea in wooden bateaus loaded down with hauls of fresh oysters; in summer, they'd have baskets filled with live crabs. Today, all that remains of that lifestyle is a museum with its iconic red roof jutting out over the Moon River. It was Johnny Mercer who immortalized the tidal river that flows in front of Pin Point with his 1961 song, Moon River Founded in 1890 by freed slaves from nearby Ossabaw, Skidaway, Pigeon and Green Islands, Pin Point is best known as the birthplace of U.S. Supreme Court Justice Clarence Thomas. Cultural historians revere Pin Point as one of the nation's last remaining Gullah-Geechee waterfront havens.

It's here in this small community that young girls still learn from their elders to skin a raccoon and cook dishes like Lowcountry Pilau, deviled crab and saltwater turtle soup.

On a recent visit to Pin Point, we spoke with Isaac Martin Jr., renowned crab net maker, nicknamed "Bone D." Isaac praises the culinary innovation of the women here who often prepared three meals a day for their families in addition to working full time at the canning factory. "In Pin Point, you ate off the land. You'd eat crab, shrimp, fish and turtles. Fried eel was a real delicacy."

At Pin Point the past lingers on into the present through interactive displays, live demonstrations and the words of families like Isaac Martin's who have called this neighborhood home for generations. One thing for certain, the mighty blue crab still plays a major role in the life of this community.

*A Full Basket, oil by John Doyle.*

# Gullah Fixin's

The Soul of Lowcountry Food: Disya Who WeBe

When April rolls around, grab your crab crackers and line your table with newspaper because it's blue crab season! Provide wooden hammers and mallets to the diners, who then pull out the tender meat with their fingers, tiny forks, or even nut picks. Dip the meat into melted butter and taste. Everyone will be happy and up to their elbows in dripping butter with crab on the chins.

The season in S.C. begins in the spring around April 1 and runs through mid-December, depending upon your location.

Just in case you haven't heard, there are different types of crabmeat. At the top is the jumbo lump with large nuggets of crabmeat. This type is expensive and perfect for salads and garnishing fish and by far the most luxurious. Lump crabmeat consists of smaller shreds of crabmeat, requiring very careful handling to get rid of little shells and cartilage. It's great for crab cakes or for blending with jumbo lump to stretch it farther. Claw meat is shell free crabmeat that comes from the picked claws, darker in color with great flavor, perfect for sautéing and crab cakes. Then there are claw fingers which are the claws and part of the shell and cartilage attached. They are delicious as an appetizer with a wonderful red sauce.

## Food for the Soul

For inspiration, we visited the Gullah Grub Restaurant on St. Helena Island just outside Beaufort.

"I'm as Gullah as you can get," Bill Green laughed as we sat down on the front porch rockers at Gullah Grub. Bill Green settled into his rocker, stretched his legs and relaxed. Bill grew up on James Island, near Charleston, a descendant of Gullah slaves.

"Growing up there," he said, "I learned to drive a mule and a cart wagon by the time I was nine years old, hauling collards and cabbages from the fields."

It was at the nearby Middleton Plantation, during the 1970's, that he learned to cook with the late grand dame of Southern cooking, Miss Edna Lewis.

"I'm probably the only one around who could follow her way of freehand cooking."

Today, he encourages African-Americans on St. Helena's to start planting gardens again and to become more self-sufficient.

## Gullah Fixin's

Chef Bill Green, of Gullah Grub Restaurant near Beaufort, calls this "smilin' food" 'cause he says, "You gonna smile when you eat it." I think you will agree when you read and prepare the following recipes for your loved ones. They are Gullah all the way food for the soul, cooked in Gullah kitchens for generations.

*Near Woodville*, oil by Clark Hullings.

*The food-ways of the Southeastern coast were painstakingly carved out of the land and water by West Africans, who were brought here as slaves generations ago.*

# Shout Hallelujah Crab Fried Rice

Whenever crab is not available, use the freshest shrimp you can find.

### SERVES 4-6

**Gullah cooks are the originators of South Carolina's farm-to-table movement,** and using the same local, seasonal ingredients and cooking techniques of their ancestors, the new generation of Gullah/Geechees are propelling the time-honored dishes of their storied past into the mainstream.

### INGREDIENTS

1 ½ cups uncooked rice

2 ¼ cups warm water

salt

2-3 strips bacon, diced

¼ cup vegetable oil

1 stalk celery, chopped

1 green bell pepper, chopped

1 sweet onion, chopped

2 pounds claw crabmeat

1 garlic clove, minced

salt and freshly ground black pepper

chopped Italian parsley for garnish

### PREPARATION

Measure rice, then rinse and drain several times. In stockpot, bring rice, water and salt to a boil. Cover and allow to simmer until the rice is done and the water is absorbed, about 20 minutes.

Fry diced bacon in a skillet, remove from pan and set aside. Add oil to the bacon fat in the skillet. Heat. Add celery, bell pepper, and onion.

Sauté until onions are clear, then add crab and cook until crab begins to brown, about 5 to 10 minutes. Add diced bacon, cooked rice and garlic.

Add salt and freshly ground black pepper to taste and stir until thoroughly combined. Cover and simmer for at least 10 minutes.

Garnish with chopped parsley and serve warm.

### TIP

*If crabmeat is not so fresh, give it added kick with a touch of Worcestershire or soy sauce.*

*"Art is more about the artistic soul of the artist than the subject." John C. Doyle*

# Crab, Shrimp and Okra Gumbo

Inspired by Gullah Grub Restaurant, St. Helena Island.

**SERVES 10-12**

**This is a big, wonderful, messy meal to serve on chilly fall nights,** when crab and shrimp are plentiful. Louisiana may claim gumbo, which is a West African word for okra, but in fact, okra entered South Carolina with the slave trade long before Louisiana was settled by Europeans.

### INGREDIENTS

⅔ cup vegetable oil

1 ½ pounds fresh okra, cut crosswise into ¼ inch slices

½ cup all-purpose flour

4 cups onion, chopped

2 cups green bell pepper, chopped

2 cups celery, chopped

1 clove garlic, minced

1 teaspoon dried thyme

1 teaspoon dried oregano

a pinch of cayenne

Kosher salt and freshly ground black pepper

2 cups tomatoes, chopped

1 pound Andouille sausage, cut crosswise into ¼ inch slices

1 pound lump crabmeat

2 ½ quarts stock (recipe below)

2 pounds shrimp, peeled and deveined

3 tablespoons fresh parsley, chopped

### PREPARATION

In a cast iron or heavy bottomed skillet, heat ⅓ cup of oil. Add okra and cook, stirring with a wooden spoon, until the okra is browned and cooked through, about 10 minutes. Transfer okra to a platter and set aside. Stir fry onion, bell pepper and celery until tender.

Heat remaining oil in a large stockpot over high heat. Reduce the heat to medium-low and add flour. Make a roux by stirring in the flour until it is coffee colored.

Once roux is ready, add onions, bell peppers, celery, garlic, thyme, cayenne, dried oregano, salt and pepper.

Stir vegetables and seasoning together. Add reserved okra, tomatoes, sausage, and the crabmeat. Stir for a few minutes, then add the shrimp stock. Bring the mixture to a boil, reduce heat to medium-low, and simmer for about 2 hours.

Add shrimp and parsley just before serving and allow to simmer about 5 more minutes. Serve over rice in deep bowls.

## STOCK RECIPE

### INGREDIENTS

3 tablespoons vegetable oil

shells from 2 pounds of shrimp

2 tablespoons tomato paste

2 quarts clam juice

1 onion, chopped

3 celery ribs, chopped

1 carrot, chopped

8 bay leaves

### PREPARATION

In a stockpot, heat oil. Add shrimp shells and cook over high heat until they start to brown.

Add tomato paste and cook until it begins to stick to the pot, 2 minutes.

Add clam juice, onion, celery, carrot and bay leaves and bring to a boil.

Simmer over moderately low heat for 25 minutes. Strain stock into a heatproof bowl.

## Appetizers for Autumn Gatherings

*Magnificent autumn! Crisp air, colorful leaves, golden marsh, sweaters and boots, football, pumpkins and coffee!*

Creating a special environment for a party is one of the most exciting things a host or hostess can do for guests. I love that feeling of anticipation while waiting for guests to arrive. I love that "ahh" moment when they get their first glimpse of the table filled with great food and decorations. And who can resist celebrating with the vivid colors of bittersweet, bright orange pumpkins, squash, red apples and rustic pears. This autumn table will delight the senses and set the stage for an evening to remember.

No matter what time of the year, appetizers should be provocative, coax the appetite, not satiate it. They might be compared to the tantalizing first chapter of a novel that immediately captivates and compels the reader to turn page after page.

*Tablescape designed & styled by Beth Blalock.*

# Isle of Palms Crab Dip

Better make "a gracious plenty" as we say in the South. Your guests will be coming back for more!

SERVES 8-10

INGREDIENTS

2 (8 ounce) packages cream cheese, softened

1 (4.5 ounce) can chopped green chilies, drained

1 cup seeded and chopped tomato

1 small garlic clove, minced

¼ cup whipping cream

1 teaspoon Worcestershire sauce

2 tablespoons fresh lemon juice

1 teaspoon hot sauce

¼ teaspoon kosher salt

freshly ground black pepper

dash of red pepper

1 pound fresh jumbo lump crabmeat, drained

Garnish with fresh parsley, chopped

PREPARATION

Combine all ingredients except crab in a large nonstick skillet and place over low heat. Cook while stirring until mixture is smooth and bubbly.

Gently fold in crabmeat. Transfer to a serving bowl and garnish. Serve with your favorite crackers of toasted baquettes.

## Artist Nancy Rhett's Remembrances

"In the words of a true Southern lady whose family has been in the Lowcounty since the 1600's."

---

**Growing up here in post-war Lowcountry,** we saw crabbers of all types constantly working the creeks in small wooden boats. The men would set out trot lines baited with potent smelling meat. The lines were marked with floats on which their particular license number was painted. Heaven forbid anyone was caught poaching! Wars were started over this for men's livelihoods were at stake.

The man at the stem motor had to be quite skilled at working the tide and the current, allowing the person in the bow to follow the trot line to the next bait line. With great expertise, he'd pull the line, then used his wire dip net to scoop up the crab, or crabs, if he was lucky. He'd flip them into a fifty-five gallon drum which, when filled, was taken to Blue Channel, the crab processing plant in Port Royal or to the Miss Mary, the company's pick-up boat. In the winter, they'd have a fire in a steel drum on board the boat to keep them warm.

It was a big industry and our local crabmeat was shipped worldwide. Because of the Lowcountry's extreme tides and rich, saline water, our crabs are already very flavorful and tasty. Ours are different altogether from those north of here in the Chesapeake Bay where water is diluted by many freshwater rivers emptying into it.

Crabbing in our creeks has changed from the thriving, big business that it was. Nowadays, the professional crabbers are fewer and the method has become mechanized. Wire crab traps, or pots, have replaced the trot lines. Winches are used to pull the haul. And Fiberglas has replaced homemade cypress and pine boats.

To see crabbers pulling their pots is a treat, and a bit of nostalgia.

*Nancy Ricker Rhett*

*Pullin Pots*, watercolor by Nancy Ricker Rhett.

## My Front Porch

"Awake to the sounds of running winches as crabbers pull their early morning bounty"

Our home in Beaufort sat on the very tip of Lady's Island surrounded by the Beaufort River. Tall white columns supported the structure while ancient live oaks surrounded it. The porch became my favorite breakfast spot where I watched the crabbers stop by each morning to empty their traps, then race off full-throttle down the river to the next set.

Our waterways were lined with floats that marked a crabber's territory. Whenever we climbed aboard our boat we'd follow the white floats and know we were in the channel, but had to be very careful not to get crab lines caught in the boat's propeller.

Crabbers go out in all kinds of tough circumstances to earn their living – fighting tide, winds, currents, no-see-ums, scorching sun and heat, ice cold temperatures and fouling seas.

Often they find their traps are empty because they've been pirated. Wars have been fought over this. But on a good day the pots are heavy and full of crabs. If pots are not emptied daily, the crabs turn on each other and die and the pots will fill with sand and become impossible to lift.

### Crab Traps

Crab traps are made of coated wire mesh with an interior compartment for the bait, usually dead fish or chicken necks. To get to the bait, a crab has to enter a one-way corridor, no backing out. Traps are hauled to the surface, swung around on board, and dumped into a basket. Then they are taken quickly to the dock and put on ice to be marketed.

*Morning on the Piazza*, oil by Helen Beacham.

# Savannah Crab Mornay Dip

This is a creamy smooth dip you will be proud to serve. It's easy yet elegant. It can even be served in prepared pastry shells for a light lunch.

SERVES 6-10

## INGREDIENTS

½ cup butter, softened

1 bunch green onions, chopped

2 tablespoons all-purpose flour

2 cups heavy cream

1 cup freshly grated Gruyere

2 tablespoons dry sherry

¼ teaspoon dry sherry

¼ teaspoon kosher salt

pinch cayenne pepper

1 pound fresh jumbo lump crabmeat

½ cup flat leaf parsley, chopped toast points

## PREPARATION

Use a heavy bottomed saucepan to melt butter over medium-high heat. Add onions and sauté until tender, about 3 minutes. Whisk in flour and cook while stirring continually for 2 minutes.

Add cream, and cook whisking until smooth and sauce begins to bubble. Remove from heat, and stir in cheese until smooth. Stir in sherry, salt and pepper.

Gently fold in crabmeat and parsley. Keep warm until ready to serve. Serve with toast points.

*Tip: A slow cooker is a good way to keep it warm. I add sherry to mine as the "secret ingredient."*

### CRABBY FACTS

**Blue crabs are not awe-inspiring and loveable like porpoises,** *splendid like marlins or formidable like sharks. They are small, quick, aggressive and feisty.*

*Ever wondered where all those crabs disappear to in winter? Blue crabs retreat to deep water and burrow into the muddy or sandy bottom to lie dormant until waters begin to warm in early spring.*

**If you have ever noticed softball-sized Styrofoam spheres bobbing in the waves,** *you have seen the distinctive markers for crab traps set in a number of area inland rivers. Crab traps are typically made of wire and are set with bait to attract these bottom-dwelling members of our local ecosystem.*

**Scavengers at heart, crabs scour riverbeds in search of food.** *No licenses or permits are required to catch crabs unless you plan to set more than two traps. Atlantic Blue Crabs tend to be the most plentiful and easiest crabs to catch and they tend to congregate around docks or along muddy banks and can be caught from the shore or from the river.*

*Pullin the Pots, watercolor by Nancy Ricker Rhett.*

*Off the Docks of Gay Seafood, St. Helena Island, SC.*

# Colleton Crab Melts

This recipe was inspired by the magnificent Colleton River that meanders through the Lowcountry.

SERVES 8

## INGREDIENTS

16 slices sourdough bread

¾ cup mayonnaise

¾ teaspoon lemon zest

3 ½ tablespoons chopped fresh dill, divided

½ teaspoon salt

1 pound lump crabmeat, drained

2 tablespoons red onion, chopped fine

32 Roma tomato slices

1 cup Gruyere cheese, grated

freshly ground black pepper

## PREPARATION

Preheat broiler. Using a rimmed baking sheet, arrange bread slices in a single layer. Place 1 minute or so under the broiled and toast each side until browned.

In a bowl, whisk together mayonnaise, lemon zest, 3 tablespoons dill, and ¼ teaspoon salt. In another bowl, combine crab, onion, ¼ teaspoon salt and combine.

Add 2 tablespoons mayonnaise mixture to bowl and stir gently.

Spread remaining mayonnaise mixture evenly over toasts. Divide crab mixture evenly over toasts. Top with tomato slices and cheese. Broil several minutes until cheese melts.

Allow to cool slightly and divide each piece of toast into 4 sections for easy handling. Sprinkle with a little black pepper and ½ tablespoon dill and serve. Positively delicious!

# Crab and Corn Fritters

Inspired by the South Carolina Yacht Club, Hilton Head, S.C.

SERVES 4-6

**These dangerously addictive little morsels have fueled countless Southern gatherings through the years.** You are likely to have all the ingredients on hand except for the crab. Picture on the opposite page is the South Carolina Yacht Club; lighted for Christmas.

### INGREDIENTS

½ pound jumbo lump crab meat

2 ears sweet corn

½ cup red pepper, diced small

½ cup red onion, diced small

1 tablespoon garlic, minced

2 tablespoons parsley, chopped fine

3 tablespoons grape seed oil

### PREPARATION

Heat oil in a heavy bottomed skillet over medium-high heat. Add onion and bell pepper. Cook for 3 minutes until translucent.

Add garlic and parsley and cook for 1 minute. Remove from heat. Drain liquids. Let cool.

In a large mixing bowl, combine batter, onion mixture, crab meat and corn. Heat 3 tablespoons grape seed oil in a heavy bottomed skillet over medium heat.

Carefully spoon batter into skillet, using spoon to shape batter into small cakes.

Cook through and brown fritters on each side. Remove from skillet and place on paper towel line plate.

## FRITTER BATTER

### INGREDIENTS

1 cup all-purpose flour

½ cup coarse wheat flour

1 cup milk

1 egg, beaten

salt and freshly ground black pepper

### PREPARATION

In a medium bowl combine all-purpose flour, wheat flour, milk, egg, salt and pepper. Stir until thoroughly combined.

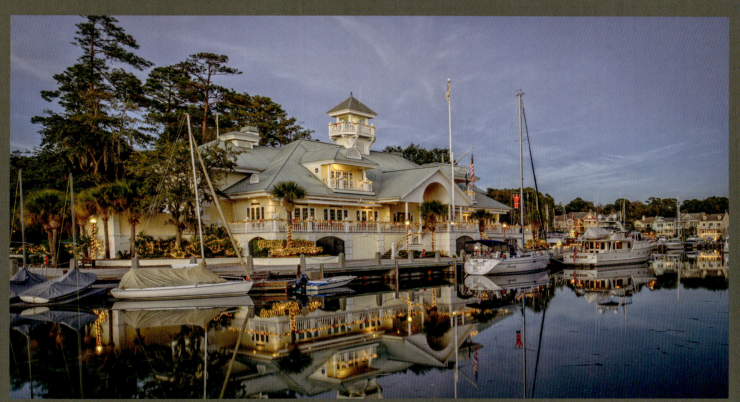

*South Carolina Yacht Club*

# Sea Island Crab Au Gratin

Delicious as an appetizer or a side dish.

SERVES 10-12

**Serve with a nice Pinot Grigio.** It was Andre Simon, connoisseur, writer and contributor to "the art of good living," who said; "Wine makes every meal an occasion, every table more elegant, every day more civilized." The ultimate alfresco setting is a late afternoon on the beach with a light breeze blowing, listening to the waves rolling in. Enjoy this delightful Sea Island Crab Au Gratin as the sun sets and glasses are raised in a toast to another beautiful day in our beloved sea islands.

### INGREDIENTS

1 pound crab meat

2 tablespoons cornstarch

1 cup half and half

1 egg yolk

salt to taste

¼ cup Parmesan cheese, grated

¼ cup Swiss cheese, grated

paprika

### PREPARATION

Sauté crab in butter for 3 minutes. Mix cornstarch, half and half, egg yolk, and salt. Gently stir into crab until thickened.

Mix in cheese and pour into buttered 2 quart baking dish. Heat at 350° for 20 minutes. Serve on avocado, toast, or in pastry cups. Sprinkle lightly with paprika on top for color.

*Crabbin'*, watercolor by William Rhett III.

*Matanzas Walkover*, oil by C Ford Riley.

# Charlie's Crab Stuffed Shrimp
## Charlie's L' Etoile Vert

**SERVES 10-12**

**Charlie's L' Etoile Vert, Hilton Head Island** is a restaurant I have loved for many years for its outstanding food and wine, but the bonus is the people who own and operate it. Charlie Colson is straight-faced and funny, and knows how to please the crowds. Their amazing crab-stuffed shrimp is a favorite and on this day was prepared just right.

### INGREDIENTS

24 jumbo shrimp, peeled and deveined

½ pound lump crabmeat

1 cup Ritz crackers, crushed

½ teaspoon Old Bay seasoning

¼ teaspoon Cajun seasoning

pinch of Kosher salt

¼ teaspoon freshly ground black pepper

1 teaspoon fresh parsley, chopped

1 stick butter, melted

### PREPARATION

First, peel, devein and butterfly two dozen shrimp. Leave the end tip of the tail on for a gorgeous presentation. Once butterflied, begin by placing stuffing on them. Do this on a sheet pan that has been sprayed with non-stick spray.

Preheat oven to 375°. Spray a large sheet pan with non-stick cooking spray and set aside. Peel and devein the shrimp, leaving the very tale tip intact.

Butterfly shrimp, rinse and drain. Be sure to remove any cartilage or shells from the crab and set aside.

Mix together crushed crackers, Old Bay, Cajun seasoning, salt, pepper and parsley. Stir in melted butter and mix until thoroughly combined.

Add crabmeat and toss gently. Each shrimp will require about one tablespoon stuffing. Shape stuffing into small oblong shaped bullets and press firmly into the butterflied shrimp. Bake at 375° for 20 minutes. Drizzle with additional melted butter, if desired.

*Tip: Peel the shrimp by pulling off the legs. Use your thumbs to crack the shell open along the underside. Pull off the shell and you're done. Devein by using a small, sharp knife. Cut from the head to the tail of the back (curved side) of the shrimp, cutting about halfway through the shrimp. Using the top of the knife, carefully remove the vein, using your fingers to pull it out if necessary. Repeat with the remaining shrimp.*

# Charleston's Meeting Street Crab

Visit this charming city as often as you can. It's one of endless delights just waiting to be discovered.

**SERVES 10-12**

**Certain recipes in the definitive mid-century cookbook,** Charleston Receipts took on a life of their own in the decades that followed the book's publication in 1950. One of those recipes is this famous Meeting Street Crab. It was contributed to the cookbook by Mary Huguenin, the cookbook's co-editor, and named for the street where the family lived.

Not only is this a delicious suppertime meal, but is equally delicious as a hors d'oeuvre at a cocktail party spooned onto crispy crackers. In this recipe, I have lightened up the dish a bit by adding shellfish broth.

### INGREDIENTS

¾ cup shellfish broth

1 tablespoon plus 1 teaspoon all-purpose flour

2 tablespoons unsalted butter

2 tablespoons shallots, finely diced

¼ teaspoon kosher salt

¼ teaspoon freshly ground black pepper

3 pinches ground nutmeg

¾ cup heavy cream

2 tablespoons dry sherry

8 ounces blue crab

2 ounces extra-sharp white cheddar cheese, grated

paprika for dusting

toast for serving

### PREPARATION

Preheat the broiler.

In a saucepan, heat broth over high heat until it simmers. Put flour in a small bowl. Spoon 3 tablespoons broth into it, and whisk until it forms a smooth paste. Pour the rest of the hot broth into a separate bowl and reserve both broth and paste.

Return the saucepan to the heat and melt butter over medium-low heat until it's frothy. Add the shallot, salt, black pepper, and nutmeg. Cook, stirring occasionally, until the shallot is fragrant and translucent but not brown, about 3 minutes.

Add the cream, sherry, the reserved broth and reserved flour paste mixture. Whisk to combine. Bring to a slight simmer and cook, stirring until the cream sends up thick bubbles and is thickened to the consistency of a gravy, 6 to 8 minutes.

Add crab meat and cook just until it is heated through and the sauce coats the crab meat thickly, about 4 minutes.

Divide crab meat between two 6 to 8-ounce gratin dishes and put them on a rimmed baking sheet. Spoon the crab gravy over the crab meat just barely covering the meat.

Sprinkle cheese over the top of the casseroles. Broil about 2 inches from the heat. Once cheese is browned and bubbly, about 3 minutes, remove the casseroles from the oven and dust with paprika.

Spoon the baked crab onto toasted baguettes or serve with your favorite crackers.

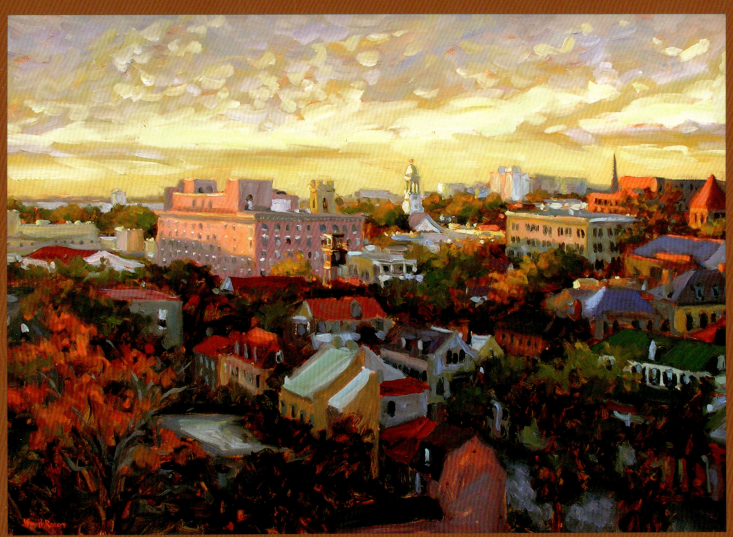

*West of Chalmers*, oil by Jennifer Smith Rogers.

## Tybee Crab and Artichoke Dip

Perfect appetizer for a moveable feast. Serve it right out of the jar wherever you are.

SERVES 10-12

**No crab cookbook can possibly be without this fabulous treat.** This is more of a spread than a dip and is best served on crusty garlic toast.

### INGREDIENTS

1 (13 ½) can quartered artichoke hearts, well drained

¼ cup mayonnaise

10 Ritz crackers, crushed

2 tablespoons pickled jalapenos, chopped

½ cup Parmesan cheese, grated

¼ teaspoon Worcestershire sauce

½ pound fresh back fin crabmeat

lemon wedges

garlic toast

### PREPARATION

Preheat oven to 320°. Combine all ingredients but the crabmeat and put in an oven-safe serving dish. Bake 20 minutes until hot and slightly golden.

Remove dish from oven and stir in the crab with as little mixing as possible, trying to maintain the lumps in the crab. It may need a little more mayonnaise. Return to the oven and cook for 5 more minutes.

Bring to the table and serve with lemon wedges and garlic toast. Delicious cold the next day.

*"After a good dinner, one can forgive anybody, even one's own relatives."*

*- Oscar Wilde*

# Savory Crabmeat Cheesecake

Inspired by Savannah's Chef Darin Sehnert.

**SERVES 10-12**

### CRUST INGREDIENTS

24 butter-flavored crackers

1 ½ cups roasted salted mixed nuts without peanuts

1 tablespoon granulated sugar

½ teaspoon salt

5 tablespoons butter, melted

### FILLING INGREDIENTS

3 (8 ounce) packages cream cheese, softened

3 eggs

½ cup sour cream

⅔ cup all-purpose flour

1 teaspoon prepared horseradish

1 tablespoon capers, chopped

1 teaspoon lemon zest, finely grated

1 tablespoon fresh dill, finely chopped

½ teaspoon Worcestershire sauce

½ teaspoon Old Bay Seasoning

2 cloves garlic, minced

¼ cup red onion, diced

8 ounces cooked claw crabmeat

1 cup shrimp, finely chopped

8 ounces smoked salmon, finely chopped

### CRUST PREPARATION

Preheat oven to 325 degrees.

Place crackers, nuts, sugar and salt in the work bowl of a food processor fitted with the steel chopping blade. Process until you see fine crumbs. With the processor running, drizzle in melted butter.

Spray sides of a 9 x 13 cake pan. Pour crumb mixture into the bottom of pan. Wipe out the food processor bowl with a paper towel and set aside to use for the filling. Pat out the crumbs to cover the bottom evenly. Bake for about 10 minutes or until lightly golden. Cool before filling.

### FILLING PREPARATION

Preheat oven to 325 degrees.

Into the bowl of the food processor place cream cheese, eggs, sour cream, flour, horseradish, capers, lemon zest, dill, Worcestershire sauce, bay seasoning and garlic. Process mixture until smooth and well blended.

Pour cream cheese mixture into a medium bowl and fold in onions, crab, shrimp and smoked salmon. Pour over the cooked crust and bake for about 20-25 minutes or just until the center barely jiggles. Remove and cool for at least 1 hour before refrigerating. Refrigerate for 3 hours before serving.

May be prepared up to 2 days in advance. Keep refrigerated

Cut cheesecake into squares and place a dollop of sour cream on top of each slice along with a small sprig of fresh dill and a shrimp or two.

Variations: Use a combination of shrimp, crab and smoked salmon totaling 1 pound. Garnish top with sour cream and salmon caviar or sour cream with capers and finely diced red onion.

### GARNISH

½ cup sour cream

fresh dill sprigs

cooked shrimp

*Tangled*, watercolor by Nancy Ricker Rhett.

## Sandlapper Crabmeat Hush Puppies

Hushpuppies are made extra special with the addition of lump crabmeat fried in a buttermilk cornmeal batter.

SERVES 10-15

INGREDIENTS

3 cups buttermilk cornmeal mix

1 cup self-rising flour

1 teaspoon baking soda

2 teaspoons Kosher salt

3 teaspoons freshly ground black pepper

1 cup green onions, chopped

2 ½ cups buttermilk

1 pound lump crabmeat

1 egg, beaten

PREPARATION

Combine ingredients together and drop by teaspoon into a deep fryer at 375° until golden and crispy.

To easily pick out any shell, spread crab on a baking sheet in a single layer and place in a 200° oven for 3 minutes. The shell will be visible and easy to pick out.

*Tip*

Purchasing crab - If you live in a part of the country where it's impossible to purchase fresh blue crabmeat, it's fine to use refrigerated canned crabmeat. Most, if not all, of the commercial crab sold is steamed as soon as possible after it is caught, picked out of the shells by skilled workers and quickly vacuum packed. It's usually sold in a clear plastic tub. Be sure to avoid Asian crab or any chemically laced product.

Imitation crab is cheap but does not have the texture, smell, or taste of crab. For best results order fresh crab from the crab capital of the world in Crisfield, Md. *www.ordercrabs.com*

*"People who love to eat are always the best people."* Julia Child

*Craig Reaves of Sea Eagle Marketing throwing pots in rough seas.*

# Crab Cakes and the Prince of Tides

*A chance meeting with well-loved Lowcountry author, the late Pat Conroy.*

---

*Here in the South crab cakes are practically a religion. Concessions should never be made when it comes to their quality, serving them only when crabs are in season. Different picking houses may produce crab that is more or less "clean," but the meat still needs a final check once you bring it home. The hallmark of a great crab cake is that it's devoid of shells and cartilage and the lumps remain intact. Take your time and carefully remove any bits and pieces of shell that remain. The effort will be well worth the time.*

We were just getting settled back into life in the Lowcountry when I received a call from Elizabeth Millen, editor of the popular Pink magazine. We had moved away from Beaufort County for a period of time and had been living in the little town of Salisbury, North Carolina. I was homesick for sea spray and sand between my toes. It was there that I started compiling stories and recipes from my life in Beaufort, S.C. back in the '70's and 80's, thinking at the time that I wanted to preserve the memory of our way of life back then for the generations yet to come. After all, things were changing at a rapid pace. It started out as just a spiral bound book, then grew into a distinguished looking hardbound book titled Shrimp, Collards and Grits.

On this particular spring afternoon, Elizabeth wanted to know where I would like to have lunch.

Without hesitation I said, "The May River Grill," knowing crab cakes there would be the freshest and finest. "Meet you there at 12 o'clock."

We both thought the story that day would be all about the success of this new book, but little did we know until later what the real story would be.

I was excited to meet Elizabeth and flattered she wanted to come out to interview me. I wasn't used to this kind of attention and thought it miraculous that this was happening. Cloide, my dear Southern husband, who has never met a stranger in his life, wanted to come along.

"Sure," I sighed, "why not. I don't think she'll mind."

Our daughter, Margaret, who was just starting her teaching career on the island found out about it and decided she, too, wanted to be included.

We arrived first and were sitting at the table when Elizabeth walked in. Motioning her to come over, she joined us as we exchanged greetings. It wasn't long after lunch was served that the door of the restaurant opened and Pat Conroy walked in with his beloved friend from childhood, Bernie Schein. Pat was best known as the New York Times bestselling author of many titles, including The Prince of Tides and The Great Santini. But to me and my family,

Pat Conroy was a friend and encourager, someone we loved for his sense of humor and his genuine love of people and sense of caring.

Cloide immediately wanted to jump up and go greet them, but we asked him to hold back. "Let's not bother him," all three of us said almost simultaneously. But Cloide and I had known Pat for many years going back in our early days in Beaufort. Ignoring our advice, he got up and walked over to their table. The exchange that took place in the May River Grill that afternoon now appears in Pat's beloved book, The Death of Santini, published a year later in 2013. The following excerpt is exactly as it appears in the book.

We have lost our Prince of Tides but the legacy he leaves behind will endure forever. Here's what he had to say about our meeting.

"Several months later, I was sitting in the May River Grill in Bluffton when a feisty, combative man approached my table. I rose to introduce myself to him. He had a terrific Southern name of Cloide Branning and told me his wife wanted to give me a copy of her new cookbook, Shrimp, Collards and Grits.

"It has my name written all over it, Cloide," I said.

His table came over to my table, and his wife, Pat, signed one of her books for me, a beautifully bound and boxed book that would look handsome in any kitchen. Their pretty young daughter had begun her teaching career on Hilton Head and had just finished reading The Water is Wide. I told the young teacher that I was 25 years old when I started writing that book and had reached the age when I did not listen to anything a 25-old, snot-nosed kid had to say.

"You had a lot to say and you said it well," she replied.

"Thank you so much." I said.

"I played golf once a week with Walter Trammell," Cloide said, with mischief in his eyes.

"I hear my superintendent was a very good golfer," I said.

"He used to beat me every time we played," he said. "Then you came along."

"I don't understand what I had to do with his golf game," I said, puzzled.

"Well, you ruined his whole life. That's just for starters. When your book and movie came out, he became one of the most hated men in America. The same school board that fired you fired him a couple years later – what you did to him haunted him to his death."

"I used to have nightmares about Walter Trammell," I said.

Cloide said, "You whipped his ass, and Trammell knew it and so did the whole town."

"Good. I couldn't be happier. But his golf game?"

"Every time we went out to a golf course, he would get ready to tee off on the first hole," Cloide explained. "Walter would begin his backswing, and I'd say, 'Pat Conroy', and his arms would palsy up and begin shaking – they would actually spasm when I said your name. It ruined his golf game."

# Pat Conroy's Crab Cakes with Caper Sauce

Recipe inspired by Pat Conroy, Food created by Poseidon Restaurant, Hilton Head, S.C.

### SERVES 2-4

**"Pat said his crab cakes were so good I would want to marry him after tasting them,"** said Cassandra King about her husband Pat Conroy. They met over food, they romanced over food and she married him.

### INGREDIENTS

8 ounces fresh lump crab meat

1 ½ teaspoons fresh lemon juice

⅛ – ¼ teaspoon fine sea salt, preferably grey salt

freshly ground black pepper

1 large egg white, beaten

1½ – 3 teaspoons white flour

2-4 teaspoons unsalted butter

small cast-iron skillet

### PREPARATION

Put crab meat in a bowl and pick over for shells. Squeeze lemon juice over crab. Lightly season with salt and pepper. Gently toss together without breaking up crab meat pieces.

In a small dish, whisk egg till foamy. Pour over crab and gently mix in. Using as little flour as possible. Form mixture into two crab cakes. Melt butter in cast-iron skillet until sizzling, and just beginning to brown. Carefully add crab cakes. Brown on one side until crispy, about 2 minutes.

Turn gently and brown the other side, about 2 minutes. Remove to plates. Serve with Caper Sauce.

## CAPER SAUCE

### INGREDIENTS

1 tablespoon unsalted butter

1 ½ teaspoon lemon juice

1 ½ teaspoon freshly chopped parsley

1 ½ teaspoon capers

### PREPARATION

Add butter to still-hot skillet, stirring to dislodge any crab bits still stuck to the skillet. When butter begins to brown, add juice and turn off the heat. Throw in capers and toss. Drizzle sauce over crab cakes and serve.

*Tip: To keep crab cakes from falling apart while you're cooking them, refrigerate them an hour or so before cooking. You can always add a pinch of cayenne for added kick.*

# Jumbo Lump Crab Cakes

Inspired by Chef Frank Lee of SNOB, Charleston, S.C.

SERVES 6

INGREDIENTS

1 egg, beaten

¼ cup cream

½ teaspoon fresh nutmeg

½ teaspoon salt

fresh ground white pepper

1 pound jumbo lump crab

Panko bread crumbs

¼ cup chopped parsley

oil for cooking

PREPARATION

Mix beaten egg with cream and spices in a small mixing bowl. Pour over picked crab and gently toss.

Add panko and parsley and toss. Cover and refrigerate for at least 1 hour. This allows the panko to swell.

Form 6 crab cakes. Heat oil in a sauté pan over medium heat. Sear until nicely browned, about 5 minutes.

Flip and cook the other side. Serve warm.

*Snob*, oil by Angela Trotta Thomas.

# Crisfield Crab Burgers

Inspired by the Maryland Seafood Cookbook, Traditional Tidewater Recipes.

SERVES 6-8

**Crisfield, Maryland — "the crab capital of the world" — is the home of this famous recipe.** There are some mighty serious crabbers in that town, and this is a serious crab sandwich.

INGREDIENTS

1 pound crabmeat

2 tablespoons green pepper, minced

¾ cup celery, finely chopped

2 tablespoons onion, minced

1 cup mayonnaise

1 cup small cubes mild cheese

few drops Worcestershire sauce

dash of hot sauce

salt to taste

lemon and pepper to taste

8 hamburger buns split in half

grated Parmesan cheese for topping

PREPARATION

Mix crabmeat with all but the last two ingredients. Put hamburger buns on a cookie sheet and lightly brown under broiler. Remove from heat and spread crabmeat mixture on bottom of buns.

Sprinkle Parmesan cheese over top. Broil 4 inches from broiler until lightly browned and bubbly.

Serve at once.

*Crab Cooked, watercolor by William Rhett III.*

# Here Come the Succulent Soft Shells

*"We have to catch 'em and bring 'em inside before they molt."*

When it's springtime in the South, it's time to celebrate the arrival of the beloved soft shell crabs. All along the coastal Carolinas, in small towns like Kill Devil Hills, McClellanville, and Murrell's Inlet, blue crabs bubble peacefully in long, shallow bathtubs. Their sweet and subtle briny flavor is like a taste of the ocean itself.

In their natural environment, blue crabs begin shedding their shells in late March. This process, called molting, allows these sideways scurrying creatures to grow larger. In this unprotected state they become soft shells, and can be cooked into a delicacy delicious enough to bring even the loftiest gourmands to their knees.

Their briny aroma is as nose-wrinkling as wasabi and the shear ecstasy that comes with them is inexplicable. I know if they were musical, they would be little Pied Pipers with people following them into restaurants in Pawley's Island, Charleston, Beaufort and on down the coast. They are a gift to us we do not deserve. They come faithfully year after year and vanish almost as suddenly as they arrive. It's best not to question why, but just enjoy until they go away, knowing their presence will haunt us with their sweetness and evanescence until they come again.

My own excitement was hard to contain as we crossed the bridge on Hwy. 21 heading out to St. Helena Island, just a few miles east of Beaufort. Once past Frogmore we enter miles of farmland still worked by native residents, many of whom are Gullah, descendants

of slaves. A sign along the side of the road reads Dopson Seafood alerting travelers to stop at this time-worn cinder block fish house at the end of a dirt road by the river. Sea Eagle Market in Beaufort is expanding and recently purchased Dopson Seafood; this new business is known as Sea Eagle at Village Creek.

"We're going to preserve working waterfront for future generations," owner Craig Reaves said.

He's a man who knows working waterfront is the most important part of keeping local, S.C seafood available.

Along the docks out front, men were working to rebuild an old shrimp boat hoping to be ready when shrimp season opens.

Once inside the cinder block seafood house I saw the blue crabs in various stages of molting and swimming around in holding tanks.

*Lowcountry Majesty*, oil by Michael B. Karas.

"They molt more often when they're small and less often as they grow," said Craig.

We captured these images while we were there showing the crabs in the process of busting out of their old shells.

"When a blue crab is ready to molt it is known as a "peeler" crab. Once it starts to molt, the crab cracks the back of the shell and slowly backs out. It's then in the soft-shell condition. This is called "busting." The time to complete this phase varies, but can take as little as 2 to 3 hours to complete the molt," explained Craig.

Rather than scour the ocean floor for soft-shelled crabs, fishermen capture them before they molt and hold them in saltwater tanks. As soon as the crabs drop their shells, they're pulled out of the water, which stops a new exoskeleton from hardening.

After shedding its old shell, the crab expands by pumping water into its body and the new shell begins to form.

In this stage the soft-shell crab is very vulnerable to predators, so they hide in rocks or bury in the mud or sand.

"We have to catch 'em and bring 'em inside before they molt, otherwise we wouldn't be able to find them in time," said Craig. "Their new shell starts to harden within about 12 hours, and then it's too late."

We left that afternoon with a dozen of the finest soft shells destined for my cast iron skillet. There's nothing better than a sautéed soft-shell crab with plenty of fresh garlic and butter. One thing for certain, they all taste better because they came straight from their source where they've been harvested for generations.

### Cleaning Soft-Shell Crabs

*Usually they are sold cleaned and ready to cook. If not, rinse crab under water. Cut off the eyes and mouth, about a ¼-inch-wide strip. Now lift the corners of the top shell to expose the gills, which look like frilly little beige pointy tongues. Grab the spongy gray gills and rip them all out at the base. Repeat on the other side of the top shell. Turn the crab over to expose its underside. There you will find a flap known as the apron. Lift the apron with your fingers and pull it off the body. Now your crabs are ready to be cooked. Put them on ice as cleaned crabs deteriorate rapidly at room temperature.*

## THE OLD SOUTH

*The scene in Clark Hulings' painting could easily be in Beaufort County on one of our many barrier islands. Beaufort, for all its turbulent history of wars and hurricanes, preserves an Old-World charm and tranquility. Almost inaccessible until the advent of good roads, the march of progress has touched it gently and many of its barrier islands remain in appearance today very much as they were a century ago.*

*The Lowcountry is truly one of the most authentic and fascinating regions in our country with a rich culinary history. For centuries, Lowcountry cooks have taken the diverse foods of Africa, France, Spain and the Caribbean and turned them into one of the most delicious and sought-after of all regional cuisines.*

Windrush Plantation, oil by Clark Hullings.

# Deep-Fried Soft-Shell Crabs

Crispy on the outside with tender, sweet bursts of flavor on the inside.

### SERVES 6

**What could be more delicious than this delicate, golden crust, encasing a sweet, succulent interior?** To serve them as a sandwich, generously spread toasted buns with mayonnaise and allow 1 crab per sandwich. To serve as a main course, all you need is a little fresh lemon juice squeezed on top just before serving.

### INGREDIENTS

8 soft-shell crabs

2 large eggs

1 ½ cups whole milk

¾ cup all-purpose flour, divided

salt and freshly ground black pepper

pinch of cayenne pepper

vegetable oil for frying

2 lemons, cut into wedges

### PREPARATION

Beat eggs together in a mixing bowl until smooth. Beat in milk, gradually whisking in about ½ cup flour, sifting it over the top a little at a time until a batter forms.

Sift in salt, pepper and cayenne and set aside.

Heat oil in a deep fryer or Dutch oven until it reaches 365°.

Oil should come about halfway up the sides of the pot. Spread about ¼ cup flour on a baking sheet.

Stir batter, then lightly roll a crab in flour, shake off the excess, and dip into the batter until coated. Hold it with tongs long enough for excess batter to drip off.

Drop carefully into hot oil, followed by other crabs, being careful not to crowd the pan. Fry, turning once, until cooked through and golden. They will float to the top when done, about 3 minutes per side.

Lift them out with tongs and place on a wire rack with paper towels underneath for draining. Keep them in a warm oven until ready to serve.

*Marshlands located on roadways often make perfect spots to pull up crabs.*

# Tideland Sautéed Soft- Shell Crabs

A recipe I love to make and learned from a favorite Hilton Head Island restaurant, Le Bistro.

SERVES 2

### INGREDIENTS

4 soft shell crabs, cleaned and patted dry

salt and freshly ground black pepper

1 cup flour

3 tablespoons extra virgin olive oil

4 cloves garlic, minced

3 tablespoons capers, drained

¾ cup white wine

2 tablespoons butter

salt and freshly ground black pepper

juice of ½ lemon

2 tablespoons fresh flat leaf parsley, chopped

### PREPARATION

Season crabs with salt and pepper and dredge in the flour. Shake off any excess and set aside.

In a large skillet over medium high heat, add the oil and sauté the crabs until soft, about 2 minutes on each side. Be careful not to overcrowd the pan.

Remove the crabs and set aside. Add the garlic and cook for 1 minute. Next add the capers and white wine. Cook until the wine has reduced to about ½. Now whisk in the butter and chopped parsley. Season with salt and pepper.

Transfer crabs to a plate, spoon sauce over crabs and sprinkle with a little more chopped parsley and a squeeze of ½ fresh lemon.

# White Boot Heroes

Photographer Andrew Branning captures the unique culture of the people who labor each day to bring us the bounty of the sea.

**White boot is a term used throughout the brotherhood of fishermen all over the world.** Coined from the use of rubber white boots to keep their feet dry and protected whether on the deck of a shrimp boat, crab boat or walking on oyster beds. Many of our white boot heroes have generational stories in the fishing industry like our friend Craig Reaves.

It's a great spring afternoon when Craig Reaves pulls his truck into the parking lot of Sea Eagle Market on Boundary Street in Beaufort, S.C. That's the day you know you'll get to eat the freshest, most delectable crab and oysters ever. And, if you hang around long enough, maybe you'll hear a good story or two. As much as I want to linger for a visit, I hardly ever take time because I'm eager to rush home to start cooking and opening those little pieces of heaven.

It's not an easy life when one has to rise before the sun and head out early to pull and empty pots, but I'm awfully glad we still have a few men who do. Craig is a fixture in the Lowcountry - someone we can count on to make our life here very special.

Locals know he and his family are the authentic articles. Their love for this place runs deep through generations, their faith is genuine and their love of life shines through in all they do. Craig and his family have been forging the marsh, rivers and streams for several generations very much like other families I meet up and down the Southeastern coast.

*The Vanishing American South:* There's tough competition from foreign markets. Our White Boot Heroes are fast becoming part of our vanishing American South, for theirs is a labor with few accolades and continuing hardships. But there's a passion men of the Whiteboot Brotherhood have in common to keep our seafood industry alive in spite of hardships brought about by rising fuel prices and imports. Being in the White Boot Brotherhood" is earned and not given. Their everyday labors go largely unheralded but these men are our heroes who enable our Southern way of life to continue.

*Lifetime fisherman Randy Higgins & Craig Reaves seen in red.*

# Crabtastic Suppers!

*Travel almost always leads to adventures at the dinner table.*

Chicken neck, a string and a bamboo pole is all it takes and you're on your way to a real crab crackin' party. The islands in and around Beaufort back in the 70's and 80's had lots and lots of blue crabs and catching them was as simple as tying chicken necks to a sting on a stick, dropping the bait in the shallows and waiting for crabs to grab hold. A tug on the line meant it was time to gently pull up your catch and scoop the crab with a net. In those days you could go out and get a bushel of crabs in no time.

I remember crab cracks from my summers on the coast — really heartwarming because they're such family affairs. Teaching my daughter, Elizabeth, to catch a crab was as rewarding as teaching her to ride a bicycle. It's that kind of wonderful experience. I'd watch as she tossed a crab line into the salt water below our weathered wooden dock. What excitement when the line pulled taut signaling a blue crab had taken the bait and was on! It happened time after time with plenty of smiles and laughter as she slowly pulled the line with a crab clinging on, wiggling and kicking the whole way.

"Be real still and pull it in very slowly," said Papa, "Now swoop in with the net and scoop it into the bucket."

Charlie, our yellow lab, danced around the bait bucket hoping for a piece of the poultry. A salty breeze swept across the marsh, offering a slight break from the scorch of the afternoon sun.

"Who's ready for ice cream?" I asked. Without hesitating a second, she dropped her line into the 5- gallon white bucket and scurried up the dock towards the house with Charlie on her heels.

Cold ice cream on a marsh front porch on a sultry afternoon offered more than just refreshment — it's the stuff Lowcountry memories are made of.

### PITCHFORKING FOR FLOUNDER

As the tide ebbs and exposes the oyster beds, flounder seek refuge in the pluff mud. They feed on finger-length mullet, then bury themselves in the mud and silt at the bottom of creeks to await the returning tide. As the tide ebbs, the water is muddy and the flounder become unaware of their predators. This is when fishermen fish with pitchforks, a custom believed to have started during slavery. The tradition has been passed down through the generations. It's a method where the fisherman walks through the muddy water sticking the pitchfork into the bottom in front of him, blind gigging. When the fisherman feels a quiver coming from the end of the pitchfork, he knows he has caught either a flounder or a stingray! Since the pitchfork has no barbs, the fish wiggles when it is lifted out of the water and can escape. Therefore the fisherman must carefully ease several fingers into the gills and, while holding it securely, raise the fish and the pitchfork out of the water at the same time. Next the fish is placed on a stringer, one end of which is secured to his belt.

# Baked Grouper with Lump Crab and Creamy Lemon Grits

The creamy topping with lump crab makes it extra special.

### SERVES 4

**According to Charlie Russo of Russo's Seafood in Savannah, Georgia, buying seafood means "buyer beware."** "There's nothing that compares to fresh, local seafood and we're lucky enough to have quality stuff right at our door." Charlie recommends asking about the fish you buy, finding out where it comes from and look for labels identifying where it comes from."

### INGREDIENTS

- 4 grouper steaks (about 1 ½ pounds), or any firm white fish
- ¼ cup Parmesan cheese
- 2 tablespoons softened butter
- 2 tablespoons mayonnaise
- 3 tablespoons red bell pepper, finely chopped
- t tablespoons onion, minced
- sea salt and freshly ground black pepper
- juice of ⅓ lemon
- 2 tablespoons extra virgin olive oil

### PREPARATION

In a large skillet over medium heat, sauté bell peppers and onions until softened. Set aside. Combine Parmesan cheese, butter, mayonnaise, peppers, onions, salt and pepper into a bowl and mix well.

Preheat oven to 375°. Bake grouper steaks for 5-10 minutes in a preheated oven, depending on the thickness of the fillets. Remove from heat and spread cheese mixture over entire surface of each fillet. Now it's time to brown the topping. Re-set the oven to broil. Broil several more minutes just until fish is flaky and topping is nicely browned. You may insert a fork to see if fish flakes and is white and not opaque. If still opaque, set the oven back to bake and continue to cook until flesh is white and flaky but not overdone. Watch closely because a minute makes a huge difference. Topping should be golden. Remove from heat. Add fresh lemon juice.

## CRAB TOPPING

### INGREDIENTS

- 1 pound jumbo lump crab
- 3 tablespoons softened butter
- juice and zest of 1 lemon
- sea salt and freshly ground black pepper
- 4 tablespoons chives, chopped

### PREPARATION

Combine butter, lemon juice, zest, salt and pepper in a small saucepan on low heat.

Cook until butter melts, add crab and sauté until hot.

Pile crab on top of fillets and sprinkle with chives form garnish.

## CREAMY LEMON GRITS

### INGREDIENTS

- 1 cup stone ground grits
- 2 cups heavy cream
- 2 cups chicken stock
- Kosher salt and freshly ground black pepper
- 1 lemon, zest only

### PREPARATION

Soak grits overnight. Skim off any hulls that may rise to the top. Combine cream and chicken stock in a pot and gently bring to a boil.

Carefully whisk in grits. Continue cooking grits on low heat, stirring to prevent sticking and scorching, 45 minutes to 1 hour.

Just before serving add the lemon zest.

# How to Pick and Eat Whole Crabs

Sounds of Gullah hymns were rising in the air with a rhythm that stretched back over 300 years to the West African coast.

---

***Cover the table with newspaper and get ready for hot crabs to hit the table. The rush is on to find the crabs with the largest, tastiest claws.***

1. To pick the crab, start by removing the whole claws and arms attached to them.

2. Peel the orange top shell off the crab as follows: Hold crab in one open palm, facing away from you. Close your other hand over it so your fingertips are touching and drive both thumbs into the slight gap between the back edge of the crab shell and the white body, then pull the two apart. Discard top shell.

3. Snap crab body in half down the middle, separating the two sets of legs.

4. Use a crab pick or the sharp end of one claw as a picking tool and prod the white meat out of the shell.

Once you've picked the crab clean, crack open the claws and enjoy the sweet dark meat inside.

## Crab Crackin'

*"Dese bones, Dese bones, Dese bones goin' rise."*

Standing in front of a mountain of shrimp, we watched as Miss Gracie headed and sorted shrimp and cracked crab at the market in Beaufort. At one point she began to sing in a rhythm that stretched back more than 300 years to the West African coast where many of the slaves brought to St. Helena Island were captured. Now, in 2016, Gracie continues to sing the songs of her ancestors - old songs with their rich histories and stories of her homeland.

# Rolled Flounder Stuffed with Crab

Delicious served over steamed asparagus.

SERVES 2

There is a wonderful restaurant on Singer Island in West Palm Beach with a marina where we often docked our boat. They were known for serving rolled fish stuffed with fresh crab on a bed of steamed asparagus. I think it might be one of the most delicious meals I ever ate.

### INGREDIENTS

¼ stick unsalted butter

¼ cup celery, chopped

¼ cup green onions, chopped

¼ cup red bell pepper, diced small

1 small clove garlic, minced

1 ½ tablespoon mayonnaise

½ cup soft plain breadcrumbs

1 tablespoon fresh parsley, chopped

big pinch grated lemon zest

sea salt and black pepper

pinch of cayenne

½ cup crab meat

2 flounder fillets, about ¼ pound each

1 tablespoon butter, melted

fresh parsley for garnish

### PREPARATION

Heat oven to 375°. In a medium sized sauté pan, sauté celery, onions, red bell pepper and garlic on medium heat until softened, about 5 minutes.

Stir in mayonnaise, breadcrumbs, parsley, lemon zest, salt and pepper. Gently fold into crab meat. Set aside.

Rinse fillets under cold running water. Pat dry with paper towels. Brush fillets with melted butter and sprinkle lightly with salt and black pepper. On a work surface, place flounder fillet smooth side up. Divide crab stuffing evenly among the two fillets.

Roll up tightly around stuffing, while keeping stuffing inside. Skewer fillet diagonally, securing the top and bottom of the fillet.

Place in a greased pie plate, seam side down. Cover with foil loosely. Bake 15 minutes. Remove foil. Bake another 5 to 10 minutes until fish is nicely browned and cooked until flakey.

Do not overcook, so watch carefully. Drizzle with lemon butter and sprinkle with paprika. Sprinkle with parsley for garnish.

# Deep South Crab Pie

Makes a lovely supper served with a crispy green salad and fresh fruit.

SERVES 8-9

### INGREDIENTS

2 – 9 inch deep pie crusts (baked 3 minutes and cooled)

1 pound lump crab meat or backfin

4 eggs

2 tablespoons flour

1 cup mayonnaise

1 cup whole milk

8 ounces imported Swiss cheese, shredded

8 ounces sharp Cheddar cheese, shredded

2 teaspoons Old Bay seasoning

1 tablespoon onion, finely chopped

1 tablespoon red bell pepper, finely chopped

### PREPARATION

Preheat oven 350°. Bake crusts 3 minutes and cool. Combine eggs, flour, mayonnaise, and milk. Mix until thoroughly combined. Add remainder of ingredients except crab meat and mix well.

Fold in crab meat trying to keep lumps whole. Pour into 2 separate pie crusts and sprinkle with Old Bay seasoning.

Bake at 350° for 50 minutes or until a knife comes out clean.

*Blue crab, oil by Shannon Runquist.*

*Summer's End*, oil by Helen Beacham.

# Seafood Mac and Cheese

Use any combination of seafood you like in this rich, creamy and cheesy delightful combination of flavors.

SERVES 8

### INGREDIENTS

1 pound macaroni

Kosher salt and pepper

6 tablespoons butter

½ medium onion, finely chopped

1 garlic clove, minced

⅓ cup all-purpose flour

3 cups whole milk

pinch of ground nutmeg

1 pound cooked crabmeat and shrimp

4 cups mixed grated cheeses, such as Parmesan, Fontina or Cheddar

½ cup panko breadcrumbs

a sprinkling of Creole seasoning, a blend of garlic powder, paprika and thyme

### PREPARATION

Preheat oven to 400°. In a large pot of boiling salted water, cook your favorite macaroni according to package directions. Drain, rinse with cold water, and set aside.

Melt butter over medium heat in a sauté pan. Transfer 2 tablespoons melted butter to a medium bowl and reserve. Add onion and garlic to pan. Cook until softened, about 4 minutes.

Add flour and cook while stirring, 1 minute. Add milk and whisk until smooth. Bring to a boil and reduce to a simmer. Cook until sauce has thickened, 2 to 3 minutes. Season with ¾ teaspoon salt, ½ teaspoon pepper, and nutmeg.

Remove pan from heat. Fold in seafood, macaroni, and cheese. Transfer to a shallow 4-quart baking dish. Add breadcrumbs and Creole seasoning to the bowl with reserved melted butter.

Place baking dish on a rimmed baking sheet. Bake until topping is golden and sauce is bubbling, about 20 minutes. Serve hot.

*Zinnias, Peaches & Sunflowers, oil by Murray Sease.*

# Crustless Sandlapper Crab Quiche

Fabulous for a brunch when served with a fruit salad and crunchy garlic bread.

SERVES 6-8

### INGREDIENTS

2 tablespoons extra-virgin olive oil

½ pound mushrooms, thinly sliced

¼ cup green onions, sliced

1 pound crab meat

2 cups Gruyère cheese, shredded

4 eggs

1 cup sour cream

1 cup cottage cheese

4 tablespoons all-purpose flour

¼ teaspoon sea salt

6 drops Tabasco

non-stick cooking spray

### PREPARATION

Preheat oven to 350°. Heat a large, heavy fry pan on medium heat. When the pan is hot, add olive oil and mushrooms and sauté, 1 minute.

Add green onions and sauté until mushrooms and onions are tender. Place crab meat on the bottom of a 10-inch quiche dish that has been sprayed with non-stick cooking spray. Spoon mushrooms and green onions on top of the crabmeat.

Sprinkle half the cheese over the mushrooms and onions. Reserve other cup of cheese for topping. Set aside.

In the work bowl of a food processor, process remaining ingredients, eggs, sour cream, cottage cheese, flour, sea salt and Tabasco, until smooth. Pour over ingredients in quiche dish.

Top with remaining cheese. Bake 45 minutes until a knife inserted in the center returns clean. Let quiche rest about 10 minutes before cutting.

*Crabbin, oil by Shannon Runquist.*

# Confederate Crab Imperial

A classic dish to serve with a tall glass of sweet tea.

### SERVES 6-8

**What could be better on a summer afternoon than feasting on Confederate Crab Imperial,** some hush puppies with crunchy chilled coleslaw and a tall glass of sweet tea — delicious enough to cause the angels to sing!

### INGREDIENTS

2 eggs

½ cup mayonnaise, plus 2 tablespoons for topping

1 ½ teaspoon Worcestershire sauce

½ teaspoon sea salt

1 ½ teaspoons fresh thyme, finely chopped

1 ½ teaspoons oregano, finely chopped

1 tablespoon fresh parsley, plus more for garnish

⅛ teaspoon dry mustard

2 pounds backfin crabmeat

few dashes Tabasco

2 teaspoons paprika

½ red bell pepper, toasted and cut into strips

### PREPARATION

Preheat oven to 350°. In a large bowl, mix together eggs, ½ cup mayonnaise, and the next 6 ingredients. Gently fold in crabmeat.

Coat a 2 quart casserole with non-stick cooking spray and fill with crabmeat mixture. Spread a thin layer of mayonnaise over crab mixture and sprinkle with paprika. Bake about 40 minutes until lightly browned.

About 5 minutes before crab is done, remove from oven and place roasted red pepper strips on top. Return to oven to finish cooking. Garnish with chopped fresh parsley just before serving.

Crab Baskets, oil by Murray Sease.

## Grilled Crab and Cheese Sandwiches

Delicious for a light supper or cut smaller and serve as an appetizer.

SERVES 15

### INGREDIENTS

½ stick butter, plus more for cooking

1 pound crabmeat, either back fin or lump

1 cup sweet onion, finely diced

¾ cup heavy cream

¼ cup Parmigiano – Reggiano cheese, grated

¾ cup sharp cheddar cheese, grated

1 teaspoon Worcestershire sauce

1 large egg yolk

juice of ½ lemon

1 loaf thin sliced sour dough bread

Thin Sliced White Bread

½ cup Italian parsley, finely chopped

### PREPARATION

Using a heavy bottomed skillet, melt butter over medium-high heat. Add onion and sauté until translucent, about 6 to 8 minutes. Add cream, Parmesan, Cheddar, and Worcestershire sauce and continue to cook another 8 minutes. Mixture should be thickened. Set aside and remove from heat.

Beat egg yolk in a large mixing bowl. Gradually add 1 cup of the cheese mixture and thoroughly combine. Stir in the remaining mixture.

In a small bowl, toss crab meat with the lemon juice and fold into the filling. Refrigerate for 1 hour or overnight before making sandwiches.

For the sandwiches, cut the crusts off the bread, and spread a layer of crab meat filling between two slices. Press together and repeat with the rest of the loaf.

In a large skillet, melt 1 tablespoon butter over medium heat. Fill the skillet with the sandwiches. Press down lightly with your spatula and turn over as soon as the underside is golden brown, about 2 minutes. Remove sandwiches to a baking sheet once both sides are browned.

If butter gets too brown after a batch or two, wipe out the pan and start over with fresh melted butter for the next batch.

Once all are cooked, spread minced parsley on a plate and cut each sandwich in half and into triangles. Dip edges into the parsley for garnish and serve warm.

Follow this up with a breezy stroll beneath Spanish moss and crystal blue skies.

*Cotton*, oil by John Doyle.

# Deviled Crab

inspired by Craig Claiborne.

**SERVES 4**

**Craig Claiborne is known as the most influential American culinary personage of this century,** This recipe uses claw meat which requires less breading than crab cakes, and the shells in which they cook help hold in the moistness and richness of flavor. I like to bake and serve them in their own shells, once crabmeat has been picked or in store-bought scallop shells.

### INGREDIENTS

½ cup celery, finely chopped

¼ cup green pepper, finely chopped

1 cup green onions, finely chopped

½ cup parsley, chopped

2 pounds claw crabmeat

3 cups cracker crumbs, coarsely crushed

1 teaspoon salt

1 ½ teaspoons dry mustard

dash Tabasco sauce

½ cup heavy cream

½ stick butter, melted

### PREPARATION

Preheat oven to 350°. Combine celery, green pepper, green onions, and parsley together in a mixing bowl. Add crabmeat, 2 ½ cups cracker crumbs, salt, dry mustard, dash of Tabasco sauce, heavy cream and butter. Toss well.

Spoon mixture into crab shells or a buttered baking dish, then top with remaining cracker crumbs, and brush with melted butter.

Bake in the oven for 25 to 30 minutes or until crumbs are golden. Serve at once.

*Memories of Summer Cruises, oil by John Doyle.*

# Sullivan's Island Omelet with Crabmeat and Gruyère

A great food memory from a trip to Sullivan's island near Charleston.

SERVES 1-2

The dish was created purely by accident. One morning as our family and friends were preparing for breakfast, one of the men reached into his ice chest and pulled out a pound of fresh crab meat. "How 'bout adding this to the eggs?" He placed the fresh crab in a large hot skillet with plenty of melted butter and allowed it to heat up. Then he covered it with foil to keep it warm while he prepared the eggs. What a great way to start the day! You'll need two pans for this recipe; a small and a medium skillet. This is necessary because the crab mixture is sautéed separately from the egg, then the crabmeat is spooned down the center of the omelet with the two sides folded over it.

## INGREDIENTS

½ cup backfin crabmeat

1 ½ teaspoon + 1 tablespoon extra-virgin olive oil

1 ½ tablespoons green onions, chopped

1 + ½ teaspoon parsley, chopped

1 teaspoon fresh lemon juice

¼ + ¼ teaspoon sea salt

black pepper

Tabasco

2 eggs, beaten

4 tablespoon gruyère, grated

3 tablespoons half and half

## PREPARATION

Place 1 ½ teaspoons olive oil into a medium saucepan, and sauté onions and 1 teaspoon parsley over medium-low heat. Add crabmeat, lemon juice, ¼ teaspoon salt, dash black pepper and 2 drops Tabasco, tossing with care to keep from breaking crab lumps.

Cover with foil and keep warm while you prepare the omelet.

Whisk 2 eggs in small bowl. Mix in half-and-half, salt, pepper, grated gruyère cheese and Tabasco. Add remaining oil to the small heavy skillet over medium heat until it sizzles.

Add beaten eggs to the skillet. As eggs begin to set around sides of pan, gently lift edges with spatula, allowing uncooked egg to flow underneath. Continue this process until egg will no longer flow when edges are lifted and is of a jelly consistency.

Spoon crabmeat mixture down center of omelet. Fold two sides of omelet toward center over crab filling. Slide onto warm plate. Sprinkle with remaining parsley.

## Spaghetti with Crab and Tomatoes

This makes for a very light supper. You may substitute shrimp for the crab.

SERVES 6

### INGREDIENTS

1 pound crabmeat

1 large sweet onion

1 pint cherry tomatoes, halved

2 – 3 tablespoons extra virgin olive oil

2 cloves garlic, minced

1 lemon, zested and juiced

¾ cup white wine

2 tablespoons butter

1 teaspoon freshly ground black pepper

2 cups arugula

½ cup plus 2 tablespoons chopped fresh parsley, divided

1 teaspoon kosher salt

1 pound spaghetti

¼ cup Parmigiano- Reggiano cheese

### PREPARATION

In a heavy bottomed skillet, heat olive oil. Saute onions until tender but not browned.

Combine tomatoes, lemon zest, lemon juice, garlic, pepper, ½ cup parsley, ¾ cup white wine, butter and 1 teaspoon salt in a large bowl. Add this mixture to the sautéed onions.

Cook spaghetti in a large pot of boiling salted water, stirring occasionally until al dente. Strain and reserve 1 cup pasta water to add to the tomato mixture. Add spaghetti to the tomato mixture with the 1 cup pasta water. Thoroughly coat pasta and season with kosher salt.

Simmer for several minutes. Add arugula and simmer another minute. Add crab before serving and gently stir until combined.

Transfer pasta mixture to a serving platter and top with remaining parsley, a little olive oil and some Parmigiano-Reggiano freshly grated cheese. Serve warm.

*Cameron Reaves pulling the crab boat off the dock.*

*Spanish Moss*, oil by Clark Hulings.

# Thanksgiving by the Sea

*Ah, autumn…my favorite season, my cozy friend who returns each and every year.*

Our table takes its cue from a wintry landscape. Decorations glisten like morning frost with a color palette that relies on gold and white. It all adds up to a visual feast. For the centerpiece, we used hydrangeas mixed with ranunculus flowers, known for their abundant layers of delicate, crepe paper-thin petals with alabaster hued roses. Linen napkins say "thanks" adding a special touch while vintage gold flatware completes the scene.

As Southerners we love our traditions and setting the Thanksgiving table is one of those traditions we look forward to year after year. Traditions weave a common thread uniting us. We love our roasted turkeys with oyster dressing, fresh collard greens, sweet potatoes and butternut squash soup. Pecan and pumpkin pies fill our sideboards as family and friends gather. Southern food matters – almost as much as our bow ties, seersucker suits and Lily Pulitzer dresses. It's tradition!

"Food is our common ground, a universal experience." James Beard (1903 – 1985) American chef and food writer

Crab Norfolk is one of those traditions that pays homage to our coastal South. Savoring Thanksgiving by the sea means including a dish or two featuring Southern blue crab. Faded now along with autumn foliage are the flourishes of summer tourists as life on the islands, towns and villages along the coast slows down. Local oystermen fill the harbors at dawn each day as perfect testimony to our ongoing reliance on our White Boot Heroes and the bounty they bring us from the sea. For all who share in the experience of Thanksgiving by the sea there is an overwhelming sense of appreciation for the South's preservation of the best of Americana and its endowment of natural beauty. Indeed, the Thanksgiving meal is but small token of all there is to be thankful for on the Atlantic-splashed shores of this beloved place.

*Tablescape designed & styled by Beth Blalock.*

*Our table takes its cue from a wintry landscape. Decorations glisten like morning frost with a color palette that relies on gold and white. It all adds up to a visual feast. For the centerpiece, I've used **hydrangeas** mixed with **ranunculus flowers**, known for their abundant layers of delicate, **crepe** paper-thin petals with alabaster hued roses. Linen napkins say "thanks" adding a special touch while vintage gold flatware completes the scene.*

# Crab Norfolk

Jumbo lump crab meat baked in seasoned butter - heavenly!

SERVES 6

**As far as anyone can tell, this dish originated in Norfolk, Virginia, at the Snowden and Mason Restaurant in 1924.** Shellfish and cured pork have long had an affinity for each other.

INGREDIENTS

1 pound lump crabmeat

1 tablespoon fresh lemon juice

1 stick butter, plus butter for the toast

¼ cup finely diced country ham or bacon

2 tablespoons sherry

kosher salt

dash of Tabasco

6 slices hearty sourdough bread

PREPARATION

Preheat oven to 450°. Spread crabmeat on a baking sheet and gently pick over the lumps to remove any bits of shell or cartilage. Sprinkle with lemon juice.

Trim crust and spread 6 slices of sourdough bread with butter on both sides. Place slices on a baking sheet. Baking for 8 to 10 minutes, turning once so that both sides are golden brown.

In a medium saucepan, melt butter over medium-low heat. Add ham and sauté, stirring for several minutes until ham is crispy. Lower the heat to low and add crabmeat until heated. If using bacon, fry the bacon in the pan until crispy and drain on paper towels. Allow to cool and crumble. Drain fat from the pan before adding the crabmeat. Add bacon crumbles and stir.

Sprinkle in sherry, kosher salt to taste and a few drops of Tabasco. Slice each piece of toast in half and place each slice on a salad plate. Spoon a serving of the crabmeat mixture on top of each slice and serve warm.

*Lunch at the Grayfield Inn, oil by Shannon Smith Hughes.*

## Butternut Squash Soup with Blue Crab

As crisp autumn evenings fall across the Southland it's time for squash soup!

SERVES 4-6

### INGREDIENTS

2 cups onions, chopped

1 carrot, finely chopped

2 tablespoons butter

1 teaspoon kosher salt

1 (15 ounce) can pumpkin puree

4 cups butternut squash

3 cups chicken stock

freshly ground black pepper

kosher salt

1 cup half and half

3 tablespoons butter

3 sprigs thyme

1 teaspoon nutmeg

3 cloves garlic, minced

¼ cup lump crabmeat

Optional: sunflower seeds and sprouts for garnish

4 turban squash or small pumpkins

2 teaspoons sugar

kosher salt

### PREPARATION

Melt butter in a large stockpot over low heat. Add olive oil, salt, chopped carrots and onion. Strip thyme leaves and add to the pot with nutmeg, salt, pepper and minced garlic. Add squash pieces. Cook until onions, squash and carrots have softened.

Add pumpkin puree and chicken stock to the pot. Stir until combined. Scoop out contents from the turban squash once they have finished cooking and add it to the pot. Simmer for 15 more minutes.

Using an immersion blender, cool slightly and blend ingredients until smooth. Stir in half and half just before serving. To serve, ladle soup into bowls and top with delicious blue crab on top.

Garnish with sunflower seeds and sprouts, if desired.

**татo CREATE BOWL** Preheat oven to 400 degrees. Use a paring knife to cut a large circle around the turban squash and cut through the turban top. Remove lid and scoop out seeds and fibers. Sprinkle inside of each with sugar and salt. Place squash and lids on a baking sheet and roast until tender, about 30 minutes depending on size. Do not overcook or your bowls will become soggy.

# Dora's Rustic Okra Soup with Blue Crab

In the South Okra often can be harvested right up until Thanksgiving.

### SERVES 4

**One of my favorite food memories happened on a late fall afternoon shortly after settling into the old Arthur Barnwell House on Lady's Island.** My new Gullah neighbor, Miss Dora, stopped by proud as she could be with a container of fresh Okra Soup. Dora lived on the edge of the property in a tiny wooden house painted haint blue to ward off any evil spirits. She stood all of about 5-feet tall and hitchhiked to church every Sunday morning dressed with matching shoes and handbag and always a large, wide-brimmed fancy hat. Other days she would go fishing and crabbing from a wooden bateau. I invited her to pull up a chair on the front porch watch for dolphin playing in the river and enjoy her soup together. I retrieved some little bowls along with a couple spoons and sat down to share this delicacy from her garden. The freshness of the okra and blue crab came through, making this one of the most delicious soups ever. Several times since that day I have tried to duplicate it, but it's never been quite the same. Hers was made Gullah style and that's with a whole heap 'o love.

### INGREDIENT

1 ½ pounds beef shank,

*cut into ¾ inch cubes, marrow bone reserved*

kosher salt and freshly ground black pepper

1 tablespoon vegetable oil

2 cups onion, chopped

4 bay leaves

pinch of red pepper flakes

¼ teaspoon smoked paprika

1 (28 ounce) can crushed tomatoes

1 pound okra, trimmed, cut on the bias into ½ inch thick ovals

fresh parsley, chopped for garnish

½ pound fresh blue crab for topping

### PREPARATION

Season the beef and marrow bone with ¾ teaspoon salt and ½ teaspoon black pepper. Place in a shallow dish, covered, and bring to room temperature, about 1 hour. Pat the pieces dry with a paper towel.

Pour oil into a large stockpot over medium-high heat, and when it shimmers, brown the beef and marrow bone in batches, if necessary, taking care not to crowd the pan. Add oil a little at a time if the pan becomes too dry.

With a slotted spoon, transfer the browned beef and bone to a bowl and turn the heat to medium. Add onion, bay leaves, red pepper flakes, paprika and 1 ¼ teaspoons salt. Cook while scraping up any browned bits on the bottom of the pan. Add more water if the pan becomes too dry. Cook until onion softens, about 6 minutes.

Add 1 quart water and the tomatoes. Return beef and marrow bone to the pan and cover. Allow soup to simmer gently on low heat for about 1 hour. Add okra and continue cooking until okra is tender, about 25 minutes.

Discard bay leaves and season with salt and freshly ground black pepper. Divide among bowl, topping each serving with blue crab and a sprinkling of fresh chopped parsley.

*Crabber, oil by John Doyle.*

## Mrs. Rhett's She-Crab Soup

Recipe is adapted from the original Charleston Receipts cookbook, published by the Junior League of Charleston in 1950.

SERVES 4-6

**No book about Southern blue crab could possibly be complete without at least one good recipe for She-Crab Soup. It is the quintessential Lowcountry dish.** In Two Hundred Years of Charleston Cooking, published in 1930, the recipe is attributed to Mrs. Rhett's butler, William Deas, who was known to be a great cook. Blanche Rhett was the wife of South Carolina Governor Goodwyn Rhett. She asked Deas to dress up his crab soup in honor of President Taft. He made this simple bisque into a legend by stirring in crab roe. This soup was served in mid-winter when the crabs were full of roe. It is the eggs from the female crab that give it its unique taste. This creamy delicacy is almost always flavored with a generous helping of sherry.

### INGREDIENTS

1 tablespoon butter

1 quart whole milk

¼ pint whipping cream, whipped

few drops onion juice

⅔ teaspoon mace

⅛ teaspoon pepper

½ teaspoon Worcestershire sauce

1 teaspoon flour

2 cups white crab meat

several tablespoons crab eggs

½ teaspoon salt

4 tablespoons dry sherry

### PREPARATION

Melt butter in top of a double boiler and blend with flour until smooth. Add milk gradually, stirring constantly. Add crab meat and eggs and all seasoning except sherry. Cook slowly over hot water for 20 minutes.

To serve, place 1 tablespoon of warmed sherry into individual soup bowls, then add soup and top with whipped cream. Sprinkle with paprika or finely chopped parsley.

#### GOOD SUBSTITUTE FOR CRAB ROE

If unable to find the roe, crumble the yolk of a hardboiled egg in the bottom of soup plates. It won't quite taste the same, but it is an acceptable substitute.

*It is impossible not to be grateful while eating She-Crab Soup.*

*- Pat Branning*

*Follow the road less traveled through centuries old live oaks all the way to the water's edge.*

Brays Island, oil by C Ford Riley.

## Special Thanks

*My books would not be possible without the amazing talent of my contributors.*

**Helen K. Beacham** - Called the "Watercolor Painter of Elegant Tranquility." Beacham's painting and teaching careers span 30 years. She is drawn to all things old and travels to Italy often to paint what resonates with her soul.

**Beth Blalock** - A resident of Hilton Head Island who created the gorgeous tabletops on these pages. She has been a gifted interior designer for many years with an infallible eye, who embraces a project, and follows through with a passion for creativity and love for all things beautiful. Beth is inventive, intuitive and lovely. She greeted every crazy idea I had with more enthusiasm and generosity than I can ever repay.

**Andrew Branning** - Born and raised in the South Carolina Lowcountry, Through his photography Andrew captures natures own masterpieces and the essence of our vanishing watermen in the American South with sensitivity and reverence. His photographs are tributes to the grace, strength and dignity of those who labor with little audience and few accolades to bring us our Southern way of life. Andrew is best known for his work on the Shrimp, Collards and Grits Southern Lifestyle series and for his large format black and white prints, depicting Lowcountry life with passion and understanding. He is the publisher of elegant coffee table books, a friend and a son who enhances every project with astounding energy, care and competence. Thank you for putting up with my chaos and showing me how it should be done.

**John Carroll Doyle (1942 – 2014)** - An internationally known American Impressionist whose artwork depicts the Lowcountry life around Charleston, S.C. He is best known for his energetic, light filled paintings of subjects as diverse as blues musicians and blue marlins. Doyle was completely self-taught. His gallery continues to operate on Church Street in historic Charleston under the leadership of the talented Angela Stump. Thank you for your exuberance, Angela, in enthusiastically sending me exactly what I request. You have shown a generosity that continues to amaze.

**Clark Hulings (1922 – 2011)** - One of the leading American realist painters of our time. He traveled the world searching for rural and urban landscapes, reflecting the vibrancy of the human spirit. He found beauty in places where others might only find misery. Hulings' ability to see timeless beauty in momentary human gestures and activities won him the appellation "master" on numerous occasions. A special "thank you" to his daughter Elizabeth who worked joyfully to be sure I had perfect images.

**Shannon Smith Hughes** – While she has traveled the world to paint, it's her home in Charleston and the surrounding Lowcountry that inspires her work. She captures the spirit of the Lowcountry in her unique way, with energy and passion. View Shannon's work at Anglin Smith Fine Arts in Historic Charleston.

**Michael B. Karas** – Master of the Lowcountry landscape. A special thank you to Michael and his wife Fern for their friendship and generosity. Your work is extraordinary and your love of the Lowcountry and its bounty serves as a constant inspiration. Thanks for adding to the fun.

**Poseidon Restaurant, Hilton Head, S.C** - Our thanks to Chris Spargur and the Serg Group.

**Red Piano Gallery, Hilton Head S.C.** - My most heartfelt thanks to Ben Whiteside for his generosity through the years and for always going that extra mile to find just the right thing again and again.

**C. Ford Riley** - A native of Jacksonville, Florida, C. Ford Riley is a highly versatile artist working equally well in watercolor, oil and acrylic. Riley draws upon on-site observation and field research to weave visual tales of the outdoors. Nowhere is the subtle balance of art and nature more richly demonstrated and keenly felt than in his dramatic paintings.

**Nancy Rhett** - A self-taught artist and a native of Beaufort, S.C. Her work is displayed in the Rhett Gallery on Bay Street in Beaufort, S.C. She is best known for her watercolor paintings of Lowcountry scenes, birds, trees and flowers.

**William Rhett III** - Represents the fifth generation of artists in his family. He is a self taught artist who lives in Beaufort, S.C. His work is on display at the Rhett Gallery on Bay Street, Beaufort.

**Jennifer Smith Rogers** - An extraordinary painter known for her images of the Charleston cityscape with her own unique, provocative style. Her work may be viewed at Anglin Smith Fine Arts in Historic Charleston.

**Murray Sease** - Shine on Art is Murray's design and illustration studio, located in Old Town Bluffton in S.C. It specializes in print ad campaigns, identity packages, brochures and web design. Her colorful paintings are exhibited at La Petite Gallerie in Bluffton.

**Angela Trotta Thomas** - After painting a Lionel locomotive as a Christmas present for her husband, Angela became the first officially licensed Lionel Train artist, a position she has held for 25 years. In 2005, she moved to Charleston, S.C. with her husband and son, Thomas. Since then, she has been an indelible fixture of the city's vibrant art scene. Thank you for your friendship and unlimited talents.

**Craig Reaves Sea Eagle Market, Beaufort, S.C.** - They were a joy to work with and I cannot imagine embarking on this project without them or doing this with anyone else. They joined us in whatever we needed to do, worked tirelessly and always added to the fun. Thank you. It was a great privilege.

**Shannon Runquist** - A realist painter born in Savannah, Georgia who has spent most of her life in the rural and central South. She finds inspiration in the Lowcountry of South Carolina and the elements of history that define it.

*Photographer Andrew Branning capturing the cover image with Vince Chaplin & Craig Reaves.*